CONTENTS

CHAPTER ONE

Another Boring Afternoon

It was one of those boring afternoons in Ashton. Ben was at his desk. He was finishing his homework – it wasn't too much today. He then put away his books and papers. He looked out of the window at the large garden behind the Scotts' house.

Ben was all alone. The house was quiet. His mum and dad were still at work. Grandma Scott wasn't at home either. She was at her judo class.

'What about my friends?' Ben thought. 'I think I'll phone Jenny and meet her. Oh, no, I can't – she's with her dad and his new wife, Tracy, this afternoon. And Nick and Debbie are shopping with their parents. What about Sita? Poor Sita probably has to help in her parents' restaurant again.'

Ben looked at his computer. 'Maybe I can talk to my friend C1B1', he thought and switched on the computer.

Soon his virtual friend C1B1 appeared on the screen.

C1B1 said, 'Hi, Ben. How are you? Oh, you don't look very happy.'

'That's right, C1B1. There's nobody at home and I'm bored. Mum and dad are at work. Grandma is at her judo class. Can you cheer me up?'

'OK,' replied C1B1. 'But what are your friends doing?'

'All my friends have got something to do this afternoon.'

'Well, what are they doing?'

Ben replied, 'Jenny is visiting her dad and his new wife, Tracy.'

'That's a pity.'

'And Nick and Debbie have to go shopping with their mum and dad.'

'I see. So you can't play football or go for a ride on your bike with them.'

'Exactly.'

'And what about Sita?', asked C1B1.

'She has to help at her dad's restaurant.'

'Rest-au-rant? What's a rest-au-rant, Ben?'

'Well, at a restaurant you can have a meal. You can eat and drink there.'

'Ah, that's interesting. But why do people have to help there?'

'You mean Sita?', asked Ben. 'Oh, Sita's dad has a restaurant. They make meals for the guests. And Sita helps in the kitchen.'

'Restaurants are places where people make meals for other people. That's interesting. Perhaps I can have some chips at Sita's restaurant. Computers need chips.'

Ben groaned, 'Oh, C1B1, you are silly. C1B1, C1B1, wait, what are you doing?'

'I'm going to a restaurant. Bye, Ben.'

There was a click and the screen went dark. 'Come on, C1B1. Stay here with me! Oh, that's not fair,' Ben shouted.

Ben looked out of the window. He looked at the garden behind the house. The garden was full of trees.

'I know. I'll do something outside in the garden,' Ben thought. 'I could build something in the garden. I know, a tree house! No, everybody builds tree houses. That isn't really exciting. But caves are cool. Yes, I think I'll go and make a cave. And it's just the right weather for an adventure – it's misty and cold; a nice autumn evening.'

Ben ran to the garage. He looked for a spade, a pickaxe and a bucket.

Then he ran back into the house and up into his room. Where was his big torch? Ben found it in the cupboard. Then he ran downstairs and into the garden. He was really excited. He wanted to make a cave. What a great idea!

'A cave is usually a big hole in a mountain', Ben thought. 'Well, we have that small hill in the garden. It's not near the house so no one will find it and it will be my secret place.'

He walked around the garden to see if he could find a good place. After ten minutes he found a place between two trees.

Ben put down the spade, the pickaxe, the bucket and the torch. Then he started to dig.

But it wasn't easy. There were stones, lots of stones. The small stones were no problem for the spade. Ben used the pickaxe to pull out the big stones.

Clank! Ben's spade hit something. It looked interesting. It looked like a piece of old metal. Was it a piece from a Roman helmet? Was it an old knife or sword? Or was it just an old tin? Ben picked it up and it broke in his hands.

'Well, that's the end of the Roman treasure,' Ben laughed.

He started to dig again. He pulled out stone after stone. Soon it was dark, because it was so late. Ben looked at the hole in front of him. It wasn't very big.

'I can't finish a cave in one afternoon. It'll take a month to finish it,' Ben thought. 'It must be really late now.'

Ben looked for his torch and switched it on. Then he looked at his watch.

'Oh, it's quarter past seven. I'll have to stop and go back to the house'. Ben was worried. 'Grandma Scott will be back from her judo class. And mum and dad will be home from work, too. It's almost time for dinner.'

Ben collected the spade, the pickaxe, and the bucket and took them back to the garage.

With his torch he took a last look at his 'cave'.

CHAPTER TWO

Ben's little secret

But what was that? Usually the stones here were dark grey and brown. But there in the hole in front of him was something that was a different colour. It was grey and yellow.

Ben dropped the spade, the pickaxe and the bucket. He went nearer and looked at the stone. It wasn't a normal stone!

Ben dug with his hands. He dug fast. The thing was smooth. Ben pulled it, but it didn't move. Ben dug again.

Finally he pulled it out and picked it up.

'I have to be very careful!' he thought, 'I mustn't break it.'

In the light of his torch he cleaned the thing. It was like a ball, but it was oval. It looked like an egg. It looked like an egg, but it was really big. And it was heavy.

Ben was excited.

He left the spade, the pickaxe and the bucket. Then he took his torch and the egg, and went back into the house.

'Ben, Be-en! Come down for dinner,' shouted Grandma.

Ben was upstairs in his room. The 'egg' was in front of him, on the bed. It was clean and smooth. Yes, it really looked like an egg.

'Ben! Come downstairs at once!' This time it was his mum.

Ben put the egg under his bed. Then he jumped up. When he got to the door he turned round.

'Great, no one can see the egg now. It's safe under my bed.'

Grandma Scott, mum and dad looked at Ben as he came into the dining room. They were angry.

His dad asked, 'Ben, what's wrong with you? You're never late for dinner!'

'Oh, Dad, it's nothing. I was a bit tired, and I fell asleep.'

Grandma Scott said, 'But you weren't in your room when I came home from my judo class.'

'Oh, wasn't I? Maybe I was in the garage, er, yes, because of my bike.'

His mum said, 'I went into the garage, and I didn't see you there. But I saw that the door to the garden was open and that the pickaxe was missing.

'Were you playing with the pickaxe, Ben?' asked his dad. 'You know it can be dangerous.'

Grandma Scott quickly said, 'Oh, I think I left it in the garden this morning. Now, have your dinner, everyone. I hope you like it ...'

'Grandma is great,' Ben thought. He knew that she was not at home that morning. She was jogging in the park. Grandma Scott just looked at him and smiled.

Grandma continued, 'I hope you like your dinner. It's some new food from the supermarket. I saw the advert on TV and thought, why not try some of this new food?

Ben said, 'Ah, I know it. It's the advert with the happy family around the table!? I hate it. It's so stupid!'

'Mmh, but the food is really great. I like it,' said his mum.

Ben liked the food, too. He liked it not only because it was really good. He also liked it because his parents did not ask him any more questions – they were talking about the food.

Ben thought about his little secret upstairs in his room. He was hungry, but he couldn't eat. He was so excited.

'Ben, is there something wrong with you?' his mother asked. 'You're not eating. And your cheeks are hot and red.'

'Oh, don't worry, Mum. I'm alright. It's just I'm not hungry. Grandma gave me some sandwiches for lunch at school. And one of the kids in our class brought in a large bag of sweets.'

'Oh, I see. So, that's it – sweets!' said his mum. 'I really don't know! You eat too many bad things. And what was the rest of the day like, Ben?'

'Oh it was one of those normal days at school, and after school …' Ben stopped, looked at his mum and smiled. And his mum smiled, too. '… I played computer games.'

Back in his room Ben got the egg from under his bed. He put it on his desk, sat down on the chair and looked at the strange thing.

'What on earth can it be?' he thought. 'It looks really strange. It can't be a normal stone. It looks like an egg. But it's very big, too big for a normal egg. It must be the egg of a big animal then, a very big animal. Bird eggs aren't that big …'

Ben turned the egg round and round.

'Well, people sometimes find the petrified eggs of dinosaurs. And they were big. Perhaps it's a petrified dinosaur egg!' he thought.

Ben was suddenly very excited. He jumped up.

'Wasn't there an article in a pet magazine last month? Yes, I remember, it was in one of Jenny's pet magazines. She gave it to me two weeks ago for a school project. Gosh, where's that magazine now?'

Ben looked everywhere. He looked in every drawer of his desk, and he looked in his cupboard. He looked through the large piles of computer magazines, but he couldn't find the pet magazine!

'Perhaps I gave it back to Jenny. I must try and phone her. Maybe she's back home now from her visit to her dad and his new wife,' Ben thought.

He left the room. 'Careful! I mustn't make a noise! I don't want to answer dad and mum's questions again.'

Ben went downstairs.

He heard the TV in the living-room. His mum and Grandma were there. 'Great, they're watching their weekly soap on TV. And dad? Oh, yes, I can hear him in the kitchen. So, nobody is in the study, and I can phone from there.'

CHAPTER THREE

Ben needs information

Ben opened the door of his father's study and quietly went in. Then he closed the door carefully. He didn't switch the main light on. He walked in the darkness and felt his way towards his dad's desk. He felt the shelf and then the table. Ouch! He hit his leg against the chair! He then found the lamp on the desk and switched it on.

Ah, yes, there was dad's telephone.

He picked up the phone and dialled the Snows' telephone number.

'Chester 384406', replied a voice.

'Hi, this is Ben. Is that you, Jenny?'

'No, it's Sally. Hi, Ben. Aren't you in bed yet?'

'Oh, come on, Sally. Don't be silly, it's only nine o'clock.'

'Sorry,' replied Sally. 'Why are you phoning so late? Have you got problems with your homework?'

'No, I just want to talk to Jenny. Is she there?

'Yes, of course she is. We were at our dad's house this afternoon, and ...'

'Sorry, Sally,' interrupted Ben. 'I really do want to talk to Jenny. Could you get her for me, please?'

'What do you want to talk to her about? Or is it a secret?'

'Sally, please.'

'OK, Ben. She's coming. And, Ben, why are you whispering? Oh, is that a secret, too?

'Sally!'

Ben waited. Finally Jenny picked up the receiver.

'Hi, Ben,' said Jenny. 'Nice to hear you. What do you want?'

'Hi, Jenny. It's about that pet magazine you gave me some weeks ago. Do you remember? I think I gave it back to you.'

'Pet magazine?' asked Jenny 'I thought you don't like pets. You always say that they're dirty and they smell ...'

'OK, OK, Jenny. It's not about pets. I still hate them. But it's about that article about dinosaurs.'

'Dinosaurs? That's interesting. Ben Scott wants to read about dinosaurs. Do you think they make nice pets?'

'Oh, come on, Jenny. Please, I really don't want to hear your jokes. I really want to read about dinosaurs.'

'Why?'

'Why not? See, I ... I've got a new computer game. It's about dinosaurs. And ... and I need lots of information about dinosaurs to play it.'

'Oh, I see. It's for one of your silly computer games again. Well, of course, you can have the magazine. I'll give it to you tomorrow at school.'

'Well, could you have a quick look at the article for me – now?! There was something about dinosaur eggs, I remember.'

'OK. Wait a minute. I hope I can still find it. Can I phone you back?'

'Phone me back? Yes. No! No, sorry, that's ... that's no good. I can wait.'

'OK, Ben. Hang on.'

Ben waited and waited. He listened but he heard nothing. Finally Jenny was back again.

'Hi, I'm back. I found the magazine and the article. Ben, are you listening?'

'Yes, I am.'

'OK. Here's something about the babies: "Dinosaur babies were often only seventeen centimetres tall." '

'Seventeen centimetres. That's interesting. And does the article say how big dinosaur eggs were?'

'One moment. No, I'm afraid it doesn't. But you can read the article tomorrow. OK?'

'Yes, of course. Thank you, Jenny. You were a great help. Thank you, and good night. I can't wait to see you tomorrow.'

'Ben, are you feeling alright? You want to read a pet magazine and now you say you can't wait to see me at school tomorrow. Perhaps you need to go to bed. Perhaps tomorrow you'll be normal again. Good night, Ben.'

'Bye!'

Ben put the phone down. Just in time! He heard a noise outside the study in the hall. That was dad, on his way to the living-room.

Ben switched off the small light and moved back to the door of the study – in the dark. He felt his way back along the wall. At last he found the door. He listened carefully. It was quiet outside. And the hall was dark. Great! Ben saw the light in the living-room. Then he went upstairs.

He was glad when he closed the door of his room behind him. He lay down on his bed. But he wasn't tired. He was excited. He looked at the egg in his hands again.

'It really does look like a dinosaur egg', Ben thought. 'If a baby dinosaur was only seventeen centimetres ...'

He checked the egg with a ruler. Well, it was big enough to hold a baby dinosaur.

'A dinosaur egg! Come on, Ben, you're crazy,' Ben thought and put the egg back on the small table near his desk. 'It is just a normal stone – but I must say it looks strange.'

Suddenly he remembered his computer. 'I don't need to wait for Jenny's magazine tomorrow. I can try and get some information about dinosaurs on the Internet. Why didn't I think of that before?'

He switched the computer on, and soon C1B1 appeared on the screen.

'Hi, Ben. Do you know what time it is? It's very late. You have to go to school tomorrow. Why aren't you asleep?'

'Shut up, C1B1, you're not my mother. I need information about dinosaurs.'

'Now? About dinosaurs? Ben, are you alright? Aren't you tired? I am.' C1B1 yawned. 'I went on a virtual restaurant tour this afternoon – and it was exciting. Do you know ... ?'

'Listen, C1B1,' interrupted Ben. 'I'm not interested in your virtual restaurant tour. I know what a restaurant is. But I don't know anything about dinosaurs.'

'Oh, Ben, come on, let's play "Restaurant". I'm the guest, and you're ...'

'C1B1, I don't want to play with you now. You weren't nice to me this afternoon. Now I need some information. And you can surf the Internet with me or go to bed.'

'Ben, please, let's play …'

'Sorry, it's time for bed for you, C1B1. Good night.'

'Hey, stop! Wait, Ben, oh, that's not fair …'

Click! The screen was dark. Then Ben started to surf the Internet. He found lots of addresses and lots of information. But Ben only wanted information about dinosaur eggs and baby dinosaurs.

Before Ben switched the computer off he tried to contact C1B1 again. But when Ben clicked C1B1's name, he only got an e-mail that said, 'On holiday in dinosaur land. Sorry, no computer link to dinosaur times.'

Now Ben knew that C1B1 was angry.

CHAPTER FOUR

Ben can't sleep

Ben looked at his clock. 'Eleven o'clock? I think I'll go to bed now. But I'm too excited to sleep,' he thought. He touched the egg again. Then he switched off the light.

But suddenly he had a new idea. 'If it is a dinosaur egg, maybe it has a baby dinosaur in it. I could keep it warm and try and hatch it.'

Ben needed things to make it warm. First he took a blanket out of his wardrobe.

'Now what I need are hot-water bottles!', Ben thought. He knew there were some in Grandma Scott's bathroom.

Ben left his room again. The hall was dark. But he could still hear the TV in the living-room. He could hear Grandma in the kitchen. It was time for her hot chocolate before she went to bed.

Ben crept downstairs and into the kitchen and whispered, 'Grandma.'

'Good gracious, Ben! You gave me a shock! Why aren't you in bed? It's very late!'

'Oh, I'm just a bit cold, Grandma. Can I have a hot-water bottle, please? Or two?'

'A hot-water bottle? You do look quite hot. Your cheeks are very red. I hope you aren't getting ill.'

'Oh, don't worry, Grandma. I'm fine. It's a bit cold in my bed,' replied Ben.

'Ben, I think that there's something that you're not telling me.'

'Well, you're right. But I want to keep it secret. At least for a while.'

'OK, young man. Now, where are those hot-water bottles?'

'In the cupboard in your bathroom, Gran.'

'Oh, yes, you're right. Wait, I'll go and get them. And you keep an eye on the milk for my hot chocolate, please. Don't let it boil over.'

'Of course not, Gran. Thanks a lot.'

While Grandma Scott was away, Ben filled the electric kettle with water and switched it on.

A few minutes later Grandma Scott was back in the kitchen with two hot-water bottles.

She filled them with hot water from the kettle and gave them to Ben.

'But now it's time for bed, Ben,' said Grandma Scott. 'Do you need help? Can you carry both of them?'

'Oh, thank you, Gran, but I think I can manage alone. It's no problem. And, look, your milk is going to boil very soon.'

'Oh, yes, thank you, Ben. Well, good night, then.'

Phew! Ben hurried back to his room.

'Grandma knows that I'm keeping something secret', Ben thought on his way back. 'But I don't think she'll go into my room to check!

Back in his room Ben made a nest with his blanket for his dinosaur egg. Then he put the hot-water bottles in it. Finally he took the egg and put it in the nest.

'There we go!' Ben smiled, when he looked at the egg in its nest.

He was really tired now. Well, it was almost midnight. Ben touched the smooth and warm egg once again, then he fell asleep.

He woke up three or four times that night. He dreamed strange dreams. He had to fight dangerous dinosaurs in a giant cave. Then he and Jenny found a little dinosaur in a hole in an old palace. They lowered a basket, the little dinosaur jumped in, and they pulled it up. In another dream a flying dinosaur carried Ben and all his friends to an island far away in the sea …

CHAPTER FIVE

A Hungry Mouth

Knock! Knock! Ben woke up. Grandma Scott was at his bedroom door.

'Ben, you didn't hear your alarm clock! It's time for breakfast – and time for school!' Grandma said.

'OK, thanks, Gran. I'll get up now.' Ben answered.

He looked around his room. The nest was in front of the desk. And in the nest there was the egg. It was smooth and warm.

Ben took a shower and then went back to his room and put his clothes on. Then he hurried back into the bathroom with the hot-water bottles. He emptied them and filled them with hot water. Back in his room he checked the nest, fetched his schoolbag, locked the door of his room and ran downstairs.

Before he went to school, he went to his Grandma and said, 'Oh, Grandma, you don't need to clean my room today. I know I have to tidy it up, but I can do it after school today.'

Grandma just smiled.

At school, Jenny met Ben.

'Hi, Ben. Look what I've got for you here,' she said and gave Ben the magazine.

'Oh, thank you very much,' Ben answered. He didn't want to tell her about all his Internet information.

'Can I see your new computer game about dinosaurs?' Jenny asked. 'You were very excited when you phoned. It must be very interesting.'

'Well, the game is interesting, but it's just another computer game,' Ben lied. He knew it wasn't fair, but he didn't want to tell anyone about his little secret, not even Jenny. Everyone would make fun of him and his 'egg'.

At home Ben watched the egg every day. Every morning and every night he filled the hot-water bottles and put them around the egg. And he turned the dinosaur egg over from time to time.

Every morning before school he locked his room and put the key in his pocket. Ben always made his bed, and he always tidied up his room. So nobody had to go into his room.

Sometimes Jenny asked about the new computer game. Ben said it was not very exciting. So they talked about other things. But Jenny wasn't happy. Ben didn't talk much; he was often tired. He didn't go out with the others after school. He just said good-bye and took the next bus home to Ashton.

One day, about a week later, Ben came home from school. He was alone in the house – his mum and dad were at work, and Grandma was at her judo class. But there was something different today. Ben heard a strange noise when he opened the door of his room.

And there – in the nest, what was that? 'Has Grandma discovered my secret?' Ben thought. Then he looked with surprise at the nest.

'The egg! It's broken. It …'

The blanket moved. There was something in the nest. Ben was scared. He lifted the blanket a little.

And there, in front of him was a small dinosaur baby. It opened its big mouth. It shrieked. Ben didn't know what to do. It shrieked again.

'Shut up,' he shouted. But of course, the little dinosaur

didn't shut up. He put his hand round its mouth, but the little monster bit him. It was very, very hungry.

'Help! What do little dinosaurs eat?' Ben thought. But there was no time to read pet magazines or get information from the Internet. He needed food for the dinosaur. He left the

noisy little monster in his room and ran downstairs to the kitchen.

There Ben opened the fridge.

'What can I feed it? I don't even know what sort of dinosaur it is. Well, it's a baby dinosaur. Maybe some milk and some eggs will be OK. And some bread, and some sausages. Let's see what it will eat. That little monster is hungry and very, very noisy.'

He put everything on a tray and hurried upstairs. Then he looked at the hungry baby dinosaur. 'How can I put the food in its mouth?' Ben thought.

It wasn't easy. The dinosaur bit Ben's fingers when he came too near.

Finally Ben mixed an egg, some milk and some bread. With a long spoon Ben put the food into the baby's open mouth.

Ben cut the sausage into little pieces and gave them to the dinosaur. The dinosaur baby ate them all very quickly.

'I think that little monster eats everything,' he thought.

Finally the dinosaur baby was tired. It wasn't hungry. It lay down in the nest and slept.

'Oh, what about the food in the kitchen?' Ben thought. 'We'll probably need it for dinner or breakfast tomorrow morning. And what will mum and dad think if they hear the baby dinosaur when it's hungry? OK, I have to go to the supermarket now on my bike and get some more food.'

He was lucky. He always had lots of pocket money. So he bought lots and lots of eggs, milk, bread, ham and sausages.

The woman at the cash desk smiled, 'Gosh, you must have a big family at home.'

'Yes, err, no,' Ben answered, 'we, we've got visitors from from Berlin.'

'Do Germans only eat eggs and bread and sausages?' asked the woman. 'How strange!'

'No, well, yes,' said Ben. 'We have other things at home. But they eat a lot of eggs … and bread …'

Ben's face went red and he quickly left the supermarket.

Just before Grandma came home from her judo class, Ben arrived home and put some food in the fridge.

Then he went out into the garden to his cave. 'That's a good place to hide all the food. I can't put everything in the fridge because everyone will see it and start to ask me questions about it. And in November it isn't warm outside any more,' Ben thought.

CHAPTER SIX

How to hide a hungry dinosaur baby

When Ben came back into the house, Grandma was there.

'Hi, Ben,' she said. 'Were you out in the garden? Not at your computer? That's unusual.'

'Can we have dinner soon? I'm hungry, Gran.'

'Well, we're only waiting for mum and dad.'

'Fine. I'm starving. I'm as hungry as a dinosaur.'

'That's strange. You hungry? Only a few weeks ago you didn't want to eat anything and now you're starving. Well, maybe it's just because you're growing.'

'Yes, Grandma, maybe.'

Suddenly Grandma said, 'I wonder where thc tray is. I thought it was here in the cupboard, but I can't find it. Maybe I'm getting old. I can't remember anything nowadays.'

'Don't ask me,' Ben answered and then went upstairs to his room. Of course, he knew where the tray was. It was still in his room.

In his room everything was quiet. 'Great, the baby dinosaur is sleeping. But I don't know when it will be hungry again. They mustn't hear it in the house,' Ben thought. 'I still have some bread, milk, an egg and two sausages in my room. I can feed it when it wakes up.'

Then he remembered his homework …

An hour later Grandma shouted, 'B-e-en, dinner's ready!'

'I'm coming,' he answered. 'In a minute.'

Maybe that was too loud. The blanket in the nest moved.

'Oh no, the dinosaur! It mustn't shriek.'

Ben took the rest of the food from his desk. Before the little monster opened its mouth, Ben started to feed it.

Soon the baby dinosaur lay down in its nest again. And Ben ran downstairs.

In the dining room Ben said, 'Hello, Mum, hello, Dad. Sorry I'm late for dinner. I had to finish my homework.'

'That's OK, Ben,' said his dad, 'I wonder how much you can eat tonight. Grandma says you're starving.'

Of course, Ben wasn't really very hungry. He had a plastic bag in his pocket. And he was lucky. His mum, dad and Grandma talked a lot. They didn't look at Ben very often. So he put food in the plastic bag under the table: a potato, a piece of meat, another potato, even some vegetables …

When Ben filled his plate again, Grandma looked at him, 'Ben, Ben, you really are starving. You never eat so much, and today you're even eating your vegetables.'

Ben just smiled and said nothing.

The family talked and talked. Ben had to answer questions, too – questions about school, homework, friends, just the usual questions. Of course, Ben answered them, but he got a little nervous. 'I have to go upstairs now and look after my baby dinosaur,' he thought. 'What if it wakes up and I am not there?'

Grandma said, 'Ben, you're not listening. Mum asked about your room.'

'Oh, sorry, I was …, err, my room?'

'Yes, your room!' said his mother. 'Who is cleaning your room? You always lock it. I can't go in there.'

'Oh, I see. Well, my room's fine. I tidy it up and clean it, too. It … it's a secret!'

'A secret?' asked his dad. 'For how long?'

'Well, another week or two. I'm not sure. May I go upstairs now?'

His mother replied, 'No, I'm sorry, you've got to help in the kitchen today. It's Thursday. And Thursday is …'

'That's right,' interrupted Grandma. 'Thursday is Ben's day. But I can do his share of housework tonight and he can do mine tomorrow night'

'Well, OK,' replied Ben's mum. 'What do you think, Ben?

'That's great. Thanks a lot, Grandma.'

'OK, Ben. You can go upstairs to your little secret.'

Ben ran upstairs and opened the door of his room. It was quiet! Everything was all right. The baby dinosaur was asleep. Ben pulled the plastic bag with the food out of his pocket.

'Another fine meal for tomorrow morning,' he thought.

Every day Ben was busy. He only had one problem: How could he hide a hungry dinosaur baby? Every morning he had to give his dinosaur baby a good breakfast. Later he went downstairs and had breakfast with Grandma in the kitchen. Grandma made a sandwich for him for school – a sandwich? No, Ben wanted two sandwiches, then a few days later three, and then four!

Grandma was worried, 'It's good that you eat when you're hungry. But sometimes I think you're eating a bit too much. That's not normal. You're eating a lot but you're not getting taller or fatter. I think we have to go to the doctor's with you. What do you think?'

Ben didn't know what to say.

Everything was fine with his pet. It ate and slept, and slept and ate. It didn't shriek, because Ben always had food for it. Ben loved his baby dinosaur. And he had a name for it, too – Dino, of course.

But one afternoon when Grandma came home from her judo class, she gave Ben a shock.

'Something strange happened this morning. I heard a really unusual noise in the house. Something was moving upstairs. I wasn't sure if it was a man or an animal. I went upstairs. But suddenly it was quiet again.'

'Well, Grandma,' said Ben. 'That's really strange. I'm going to do some homework now.'

'Wait a moment,' said Grandma. 'A little bit later I heard the noise again. Again I thought it came from one of the rooms upstairs. I'm not scared, you know, because I'm good at judo. So I went upstairs and it was quiet again. I think it's time that I take some extra judo classes so that I can fight anyone who wants to break into our house.'

'I'm sure it was nothing, Grandma. Just the wind.'

'I'm sure it wasn't the wind. And I think the noise came from your room.'

'Oh dear,' Ben thought. 'I'm lucky my little dinosaur is scared, too. It's always quiet when it hears someone. But Grandma's extra judo classes is a great idea. A few more hours for the little dinosaur alone at home!'

CHAPTER SEVEN

The end of a secret

A few days later Ben came home from school. Everything looked the same as usual. The house was quiet. But then Ben came upstairs. What he saw gave him a real shock!

When he opened his bedroom, his room was a complete mess. Everything that had been on his desk was now on the floor, the doors of the wardrobe were broken, his computer monitor lay on its side, his books were lying all over the room. And where was Dino?

Dino was behind the bed. He looked scared. But when he saw Ben, he jumped towards him – with Ben's football. It looked funny. Dino kicked the ball with his feet and with his big mouth. He jumped onto the ball and over the ball.

But Ben didn't laugh. 'That's the end of my secret,' he thought, and he looked at the mess in his room.

Ben was sad, and he was scared. 'How can I tell Grandma and mum and dad?' he thought. He started to tidy up. Dino went to his nest and lay under his blanket.

Soon Ben heard Grandma at the front door.

'B-e-en,' she shouted, when she was in the hall. 'B-e-n? Are you at home?' Then she looked up, and she saw Ben. He was standing upstairs with a strange animal next to him. It had a football in its mouth.

'Oh my goodness! Ben, what on earth is that thing next to you?' she shouted. 'What sort of animal is that! It looks like a monster!'

Ben had to tell her the story – the story of his cave, the egg, and the little dinosaur next to him.

Dino was quiet. It looked at Grandma all the time. Was she dangerous? No, she looked OK.

'A dinosaur!', Grandma laughed when Ben finished his story. 'I can't believe it. A dinosaur in my house. A sweet little dinosaur baby. But, Ben, your mum and dad are coming home soon. We've got to tell them. And what are we going to do with this funny little monster? It isn't a pet like a dog. We have to find out more about it. Maybe we can give it to Chester Zoo.'

Ben didn't like the idea of Chester Zoo. But he felt better now. Grandma Scott was there to help him – she was the best grandma in the world! And she helped Ben with his room.

'No, not the zoo,' Grandma suddenly said. 'Why not start a "dino park"? There was a film on TV about a dinosaur park in Germany some days ago. They've only got plastic dinosaurs. We could start a dinosaur park with a real dinosaur.'

Ben looked at Grandma. 'Grandma, that's a great idea. Do you think it could work? But what about mum and dad?! Oh, er, listen, I think they're coming home.'

Mr and Mrs Scott knew at once that there was something wrong. 'What's going on here, Ben?' asked his mum.

'What's going on here, Mum?' asked his dad.

Just then there was a strange noise from upstairs, and then something jumped downstairs step by step.

'Agh!' shrieked Ben's mum. 'What on earth is that?'

Ben had to tell his story again – the story of his cave, the egg, and the little dinosaur next to him.

Ben's dad was shocked. 'What are we going to do now? We can't have a dinosaur here in the house. It's not a pet like a dog or a cat.'

'Or a tortoise,' said his mum. 'We have to give it to a zoo. We can't keep it. And we have no idea what sort of dinosaur it is.'

‘Maybe it’s …,’ said his dad.

‘It’s not an “it” – it’s a “he”!’ said Ben angrily. ‘And his name is Dino.’

‘OK. He. Maybe he’s dangerous. Maybe he’ll eat us one day.’

‘And he’ll probably grow and grow,’ said his mum. ‘Look how big he is now! How old is he?

‘Twenty days old.’

‘Twenty days? Think how big he’ll be in a month or two! And in a year! No, I don’t want that monster here in the house.’

‘Of course we can’t keep it, Karin.’

‘Listen, Karin and Richard,’ said Grandma. ‘Ben and I have got a good idea: We’ve got a big garden. And there’s farmland behind the garden. Why don’t we buy it, and start a big dinosaur park?’

‘A dinosaur park? You’re joking. There are dinosaur parks all over the world.’

‘Yes, but no dinosaur park has got a living dinosaur,’ replied Ben.

‘Oh, come on, Ben,’ said his mum. ‘It would be so expensive. We would need a cage, a very big dinosaur house, and lots of food for that monster there.’

‘We would have to build a car park, a restaurant …’

‘And souvenir shops,’ said Ben. ‘Mum, Dad, millions of people would love to see a real dinosaur. We could sell millions and millions of tickets. And we could all work here together from morning to evening. Me, Grandma, and you two. You needn’t go out to work. You needn’t leave the house early in the morning and come home late in the afternoon.’

‘OK,’ said Grandma. ‘Let’s think about it this evening. Of course, we would need money to build a dinosaur park. But let's have dinner first.'

'Yes,' said his mum. 'And, Ben, you take that monster to the garage.'

'Oh, Mum, Dino is really quiet now. Look. I can't take him out into that dark, cold garage. He's a baby!'

'Well, OK, but give him some food. He needn't eat us then. By the way, what does he eat?'

'Oh, I think I know, Karin,' said Grandma. 'Come and help me in the kitchen, Ben.'

Ben and Grandma went into the kitchen. Dino stayed in the hall. He was tired. He lay down and fell asleep.

Ben's mum and dad looked at him, and then shook their heads.

Later they all had dinner in the dining room. Grandma made a big meal for Dino, too. He had his meal in the hall.

When Ben finally had to go to bed, his dad told him, 'Don't take that monster into your room again. We can keep him down here in the small room next to the study.'

'I must say, the idea of a dinosaur park isn't so bad,' said his mum. 'You could all stay at home and work here. And we could get very rich. Goodnight, Ben.'

Ben smiled and went upstairs.

In his bedroom Ben looked at his clock. 'Ten thirty? I think I am too excited to sleep,' he thought.

Then he got into bed and switched off the light and fell asleep.

The alarm-clock in his computer woke Ben up. He still felt tired. C1B1 was on the screen, 'Good morning, Ben. You're late. See you this afternoon. Good-bye.'

CLICK – the screen was dark again, and Ben's room was dark again, too. It was a really cold November morning. Ben switched the lamp on. There in front of him in a little nest was his 'egg', his dinosaur egg.

'Ben, come down, please. Breakfast is ready,' Grandma shouted from downstairs ...

'Oh my goodness,' thought Ben. 'Was it all just a dream?'

Your Favourite Ending

That was the story of Ben's pet. But it's not the end of the story. Ben's 'egg' was real – it was not just a part of his dream.

Can you think of an ending to the story? What do you think Ben did next? Maybe you've got a great idea to finish the story. But you can also read one of these three endings. Perhaps you can also read the other endings later. Which one do you like best? Or is your idea much better?

Ending One:
Grandma knows someone at an archeological institute. He can find out if it is a dinosaur's egg ...
Start on p. 38.

Ending Two:
Grandma tells Ben about a story competition in the newspaper ...
Start on p. 40.

Ending Three:
At school Jenny tells Ben about a dinosaur film on TV ...
Start on p. 42.

Ending One

Is it a dinosaur's egg?

'Oh, yes, the dinosaur egg,' Ben thought and smiled. He touched the strange stone before he got up. It was smooth and warm. Ben was still tired. He yawned. 'I think I went to bed very late last night.'

On the way to the bathroom, he heard Grandma Scott again, 'Ben, are you coming? Breakfast is ready!'

'OK, Gran, in a minute,' Ben answered.

'Fine, but hurry up, you're late,' shouted Grandma.

He washed his face and cleaned his teeth, and thought about his cave and the stone, 'Should I tell Grandma about it, or mum and dad, or my friends at school? I know, I'll show it to Grandma!' He thought about his dream last night and smiled, 'What a silly dream!'.

A few minutes later, he carried the 'egg' downstairs. 'Be very careful, I mustn't break it,' Ben thought on the way to the kitchen.

'Good morning, Gran,' he said when he went into the kitchen.

'Morning, Ben. Hey, what's that?'

'Well, it's a sort of stone. I found it in the garden yesterday. Doesn't it look great?'

'It looks like an egg to me.'

'Yes, it does. Maybe it's a dinosaur's egg, a petrified egg.'

'A dinosaur's egg? Well, yes, why not? Oh, we have to find out what it is. We can ask Mr Jones. He's in my judo class, and he works at an archaeological institute. I can phone him today, and perhaps after school we can go and visit him.'

Ben liked the idea. But at school he didn't talk about the

egg. He didn't even tell Jenny about it when she gave him the pet magazine. Ben could only think of Mr Jones and the archaeological institute. Mr Jones must know what it is.

Grandma Scott waited for Ben after school. She and Ben then drove to the institute.

'I phoned your parents this morning,' Grandma told Ben on the way there. 'I told them about the strange stone. And I told them about our visit to Mr Jones. He's waiting for us. He's very excited. And your mum and dad are coming, too. They'll leave work earlier today.'

'Mum and dad are coming too – on a weekday!' Ben thought. He was very, very happy.

Two days later this story appeared in the Chester newspaper:

DINO FEVER IN ASHTON

A 12-year-old boy from Ashton finds a petrified dinosaur egg in his garden.

Two days ago Ben Scott was digging in his garden when he found a smooth grey stone. He did not know what it was, but his family took it to Professor Jones of the Chester Archaeological Museum, who told them that it was a petrified dinosaur's egg.

Prof Jones is very excited by the discovery. 'It is Chester's first petrified dinosaur egg.'

The museum will keep the egg. 'I would like to keep it but it is probably better that everyone can see it in the museum,' said young archaeologist, Ben Scott. 'But maybe we can find more eggs in our garden.'

Ben Scott and his egg

Ending Two

An idea for a good story

'Oh, yes, the dinosaur egg,' Ben thought and smiled. He touched the strange stone before he got up. It was smooth and warm. Ben was still tired. He yawned. 'I think I went to bed very late last night.'

On the way to the bathroom, he heard Grandma Scott again, 'Ben, are you coming? Breakfast is ready!'

'OK, Gran, in a minute,' Ben answered.

'Fine, but hurry up, you're late,' shouted Grandma.

He washed his face and cleaned his teeth, and thought about his cave and the stone, 'Should I tell Grandma about it, or mum and dad, or my friends at school? No, I think the egg is my secret.' He thought about his dream last night and smiled, 'What a silly dream!'

'Good morning, Gran.'

Grandma was reading the newspaper, but she looked up when Ben came into the kitchen. 'Morning, Ben. Are you feeling well this morning?'

'Yes, fine, thanks.'

'My hot-water bottles are always a great help!'

'I know, Gran.'

'Now listen to this. The newspaper is doing a story competition for school kids. Why don't you write a story for that competition? You always have great ideas.'

'Mmh, I don't know ...'

Ben didn't like the idea at first. At school he thought about it sometimes. But he didn't talk to his friends about the egg. They would only laugh. He didn't even tell Jenny about it when she gave him the pet magazine.

After school, Ben was alone at home again. 'I can go out into the garden and dig my cave,' he thought. But it was cold and rainy. 'No, I think I'll go and find the newspaper. Maybe that competition isn't so bad. And I know I can tell great stories ...'

He touched the smooth egg on the bed next to him.

Ben went downstairs and found the newspaper in the living-room. A few minutes later he was sitting in front of his computer and started to write ...

A month later this story appeared in the Chester newspaper:

DINO FEVER IN ASHTON

A 12-year-old boy from Ashton wins this newspaper's story competition.

'My grandma told me about the competition,' said young author, Ben Scott. 'And then I had this idea about a boy and a petrified dinosaur's egg. The boy finds the egg in his garden.'

The winner's story is really entertaining. Lots of things happen when the boy tries to hatch the egg. He is very surprised when one day a baby

Ben Scott receives his reward for best story

dinosaur comes out of the egg. At first the boy hides his little monster

Ending 3

Jennys tells Ben a strange story

'Oh, yes, the dinosaur egg,' Ben thought and smiled. He touched the strange stone before he got up. It was smooth and warm. Ben was still tired. He yawned. 'I think I went to bed very late last night.'

On the way to the bathroom, he heard Grandma Scott again, 'Ben, are you coming? Breakfast is ready!'

'OK, Gran, in a minute,' Ben answered.

'Fine, but hurry up, you're late,' shouted Grandma.

He washed his face and cleaned his teeth, and thought about his cave and the stone, 'Should I tell Grandma about it, or mum and dad, or my friends at school? No, I think the egg is my secret.' He thought about his dream last night and smiled, 'What a silly dream!'

Later at school he met Jenny. She had the pet magazine in her hand. She smiled when she saw Ben.

'Hello, Ben. You're late. And you look tired. Did you go to bed late last night?'

'Yes, I did. I found some interesting information about dinosaurs on the Internet.'

'On the Internet? So, you don't need my pet magazine ...'

'No, no, it's OK, Jenny. I still want it. Thank you very much.'

'Your new computer game must be very exciting. Can I play with it, too?'

'Mmh, I don't know ...'

'Did you watch TV yesterday, Ben?' asked Jenny.

'TV? No, I didn't. I did my homework first, and then I played in the garden. Why do you ask?'

'Oh, I watched an exciting film on TV yesterday at dad and Tracy's house. It was about a young boy. He found a dinosaur's egg in his garden, a petrified egg. And then the boy tried to hatch it …'

Ben's face went red. 'What's funny about that? You can't hatch a petrified egg. That's silly.'

'Well, of course, you can't, but in a film …'

'Or in a dream …'

'Err? Right … Now, one day there really was a baby dinosaur in the nest. And of course, the baby dinosaur was hungry.'

'So, the boy bought some food for it.'

'Ben, how do you know? You said you didn't watch TV yesterday.'

'Well, it was just an idea.'

'By the way, the second part of the film is on TV this afternoon.

'Great, let's watch it together.'

6.30 DINO FEVER (2)

The second part of the television drama about the strange story of the boy and the dinosaur.
Ben's family decides to keep the dinosaur and open 'Dino Park'.
However, the baby dinosaur is no longer a sweet pet and becomes bigger and bigger. Things start to go very wrong! The film stars Leonardo Scott, Jenny Winslet and Britney Kingsway.

Dinosaurs do not make great pets

VOCABULARY

Abbreviations

adj	=	adjective	n	=	noun
adv	=	adverb	prep	=	preposition
conj	=	conjunction	sb.	=	somebody
jdn.	=	jemanden	sth.	=	something

A

advert Werbespot
archaeological [ˌɑːkiəˈlɒdʒɪkl] archäologisch
article Artikel
(to) **be asleep** schlafen
(to) **fall asleep** einschlafen
at first zuerst, zunächst

B

basket Korb
bit: (to) **bite** [baɪt] beißen
blanket Decke
boil [bɔɪl] kochen, zum Kochen bringen
(to) **break into** einbrechen in
bucket Eimer
by the way übrigens

C

cage [keɪdʒ] Käfig
cave [keɪv] Höhle
car park (Auto-)Parkplatz
cash desk Kasse
cheek [tʃiːk] Wange, Backe
(to) **cheer sb. up** [tʃɪə] jdn. aufheitern
complete [kəmˈpliːt] vollständig, völlig
(to) **contact** Kontakt aufnehmen mit
(to) **continue** [kənˈtɪnjuː] fortfahren, weiter reden
could [kəd] konnte(n), könnte(n)
I'm cold mir ist kalt, ich friere
crept: (to) **creep** [kriːp] schleichen
(to) **cut** schneiden

D

darkness Dunkelheit
(to) **dial** [ˈdaɪəl] wählen
(to) **dig** graben
dining room [ˈdaɪnɪŋ] Esszimmer
dinosaur [ˈdaɪnəsɔː] Dinosaurier
(to) **discover** entdecken, aufdecken
discovery Entdeckung
drawer [drɔː] Schublade
dug: (to) **dig** graben

E

What on earth …? Was in aller Welt …?
(to) **empty** entleeren
enough [ɪˈnʌf] genug
entertaining [ˌentəˈteɪnɪŋ] unterhaltsam
excited [ɪkˈsaɪtɪd] aufgeregt, gespannt

F

farmland Acker- und Weideland
feel your way dir deinen Weg tastend suchen
fever ['fiːvə] Fieber
(to) **fill** füllen
finally ['faɪnəli] schließlich, endlich
flying ['flaɪɪŋ] fliegend
fridge Kühlschrank
(to) **make fun of** sich lustig machen über

G

Gosh! Mensch! Mann!
Oh my goodness Ach du meine Güte!
(to) **grow** [grəʊ] wachsen

H

hall [hɔːl] Flur
hang on wart mal
(to) **hatch** ausbrüten
heavy ['hevi] schwer
hot-water bottle Wärmflasche
(to) **hurry** ['hʌri] eilen, hasten
(to) **hurry up** sich beeilen

I

I'll (= **I will**) ich werde
(to) **get ill** krank werden
(to) **interrupt** unterbrechen

J

(to) **be joking** Witze machen

K

kettle Kessel
key [kiː] Schlüssel

L

lay [leɪ]**:** (to) **lie** [laɪ] liegen, sich legen
(to) **lie down** sich hin-/niederlegen
lied: (to) **lie** liegen, sich legen; lügen
(to) **lift** anheben
living lebend
(to) **lock** abschließen
(to) **have a look at sb./sth.** einen Blick werfen auf
(to) **lower** ['ləʊə] herab-/hinablassen

M

main light das große Licht
(to) **manage sth.** etwas hinkriegen
(to) **mean** [miːn] meinen
mess Durcheinander
(to) **be missing** fehlen
misty (leicht) nebelig
(to) **mix** mischen, mixen

N

nearer näher
nest Nest
noisy ['nɔɪsi] laut, lärmend
nowadays ['naʊədeɪz] heutzutage

P

palace ['pæləs] Palast, Schloss
petrified ['petrɪfaɪd] versteinert
pickaxe ['pɪkæks] (Spitz)Hacke
(to) **pick up** aufnehmen, hochheben
pile [paɪl] Stapel, Haufen
that's a pity das ist schade
plastic bag Plastiktüte
probably wahrscheinlich

R

(to) **receive** [rɪ'siːv] erhalten
receiver [rɪ'siːvə] (Telefon-)Hörer
replied: (to) **reply** antworten

S
(to) **be scared** [skeəd] Angst haben
screen [skri:n] Bildschirm
secret ['si:krət] Geheimnis
share [ʃeə] Teil
should [ʃəd] sollte(n)
shower [ʃaʊə] Dusche, Duschbad
(to) **shriek** [ʃri:k] kreischen
(to) **give a shock** einen Schrecken einjagen
shook [ʃʊk]**:** (to) **shake your head** den Kopf schüttelten
side Seite
smooth [smu:ð] glatt
soap [səʊp] Seifenoper
spade [speɪd] Spaten
spoon [spu:n] Löffel
(to) **be starving** einen Riesenhunger haben
step Stufe
strange [streɪndʒ] merkwürdig, seltsam
study ['stʌdi] Arbeitszimmer
surprise Überraschung
(to) **surprise** überraschen
surprising überraschend
sweet [swi:t] süß
switch on/off ein-/ausschalten
sword [sɔ:d] Schwert

T
(to) **take (a month)** (einen Monat) dauern
torch [tɔ:tʃ] Taschenlampe
tray [treɪ] Tablett
treasure ['treʒə] Schatz
(to) **turn over** umdrehen

V
virtual ['vɜ:tʃuəl] virtuell

W
weekly wöchentlich
whole [həʊl] ganz
will werden
(to) **wonder** sich fragen
(to) **work** klappen, funktionieren
would [wəd] würde(n)

Y
(to) **yawn** [jɔ:n] gähnen